REVENGE

Lauri Robertson's *Revenge* cuts to the core of strife between libido and aggression. As a psychiatrist and psychoanalyst she asks in the preface, "In all seriousness, what does one do with rage..?" It's a painful question for our time, or all time. With intimate wit and wisdom she surveys, if not integrates, the vast landscape of internal conflict.

    Elise W. Snyder, MD

Lauri Robertson titles her book *Revenge*, and she does take on some unpleasant incidents that require responses in these poems; but ultimately the words she chooses are existential, aware of time passing and death around the corner. So why hold rancors? Why seek revenge? With a clear and easy diction she invites sensitive and thoughtful readers to answer. It is refreshing to read poems like water in a stream, to see your reflection, to understand one's common humanity and one's desire for redress.

    Indran Amirthanayagam, author of *The Runner's Almanac*

In *Revenge*, Lauri Robertson's biting 6th volume of poetry, a woman becomes so angry that she throws a piece of plastic into the regular garbage instead of the recycling. But, it's not all a revenge-lite catalogue; note the Girl Scouts accidentally or otherwise leaving her out of the troop because her mother was in a psychiatric hospital. The vignettes resonate deeply, and remind the reader of their own stories. Robertson, who happens to be a psychoanalyst, makes unvarnished, dumbfounded inquiry into our nature(s). This is not appalling, worldly revenge, though perhaps some kind of understanding begins here.

    Susan Lewis Duffy

Robertson's new poetry volume employs intimate and personal language to confront humanity with the courage and tenderness of a psychoanalyst. She wonders "what does one do with rage and aggression?" While looking for answers her incisive observations reveal the fragility, imperfections and blemishes of life. There are encounters with people who represent states of the heart, of the mind, even bureaucrats, housekeepers, or bus drivers. Those encounters reveal an aching vulnerability, "a world in so much pain." She writes: "You may not know the true / depth of the wound / until your scalpel / explores it." But deliverance can only arise from understanding, and the poems' luminosity brings us forth triumphantly. Robertson has written the book we all want to write but don't dare.

Jorge Armenteros, author of *The Curvature of An Absence*

Revenge

Lauri Robertson

Spuyten Duyvil

New York City

ISBN 978-1-963908-35-0

Cover photo by the author. "Rue de Rivoli", Paris, 2023.

Library of Congress Control Number: 2024944524

CONTENTS

PREFACE

D ecades ago I had a little collage on the wall, made up in part of *New York Times* headlines: "The Best Revenge", "The Best Revenge Continued", "The Best Revenge is Living Well" (of course), "...Eating Well", "...Writing Well", etc.

It was meant to amuse, address the pinpricks of daily life and remind me not to be too fatootsed by them. It was also a small protest against a good girl's enforced super-ego civility.

The assemblage is long gone, and my husband chastens that revenge sours one's being, and how abhorrent a sentiment in a hateful world. But, *no* I say, it's also about loss, guilt, shame, humiliation, survival, regret, lament, *mea culpa,* and reparation, at least.

In all seriousness, what does one do with rage and aggression? This 'drive' to settle the score? I'm a psychoanalyst, should I know? Make humor, make art, 'sublimate', pray? "Turn the other cheek?" What platitude can you possibly escape?

I think of Toni Morrison's moral certitude that it is perpetrators who are inferior, and damage themselves. And I think merely of the title of her book of essays: *The Source of Self-Regard...*

(I might add, for clarity @ some of the entries, that my mother was mentally ill, and hospitalized for a number of years during my childhood in the 1950's.)

"But then I realized that I had been tricked by words older than Anse or love, and that the same word had tricked Anse too, and that my revenge would be that he would never know I was taking revenge."

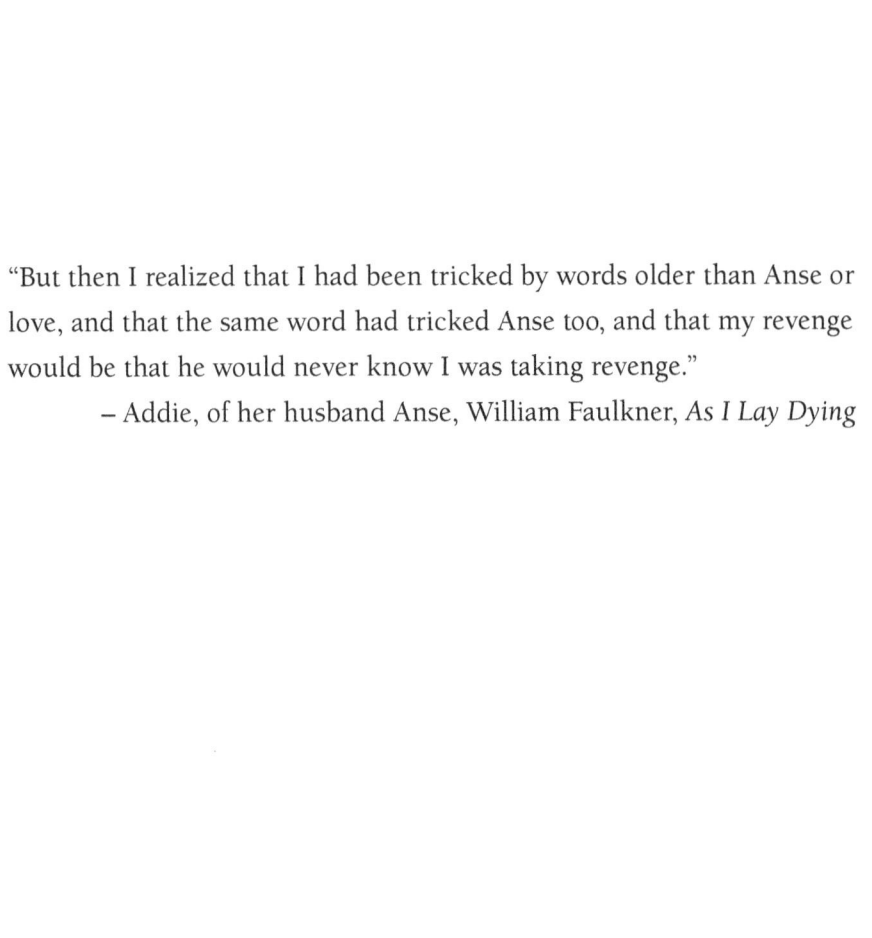

– Addie, of her husband Anse, William Faulkner, *As I Lay Dying*

PROLOGUE

Please read these...

...with the mean-spirited goodwill intended
inquiry, even the humor they deserve.

Why does it still sting after decades?
And, you know you know what I mean.

Not just annoyance, *Oh please!* or *Thanks for nothing*!
There has to be, uh, a stinger, and the right venom.

What you should have said, jangling in your head
with infinite addenda. Even if it prompted

free flight to a far better life.
Or, was inconsequential, even trivial

unrecognizable, but to the bearer of pain.
Not pain like #BLM, or The Middle East

but micro. A thorn is a thorn is a thorn:
ignoring, erasing, flinching, dismissing

looking down your long, stinking snout
for nothing? Even inadvertently, if that's possible.

Sniff yourself. Think of what *kind* and *unkind*
really are, think of your ignorance, your choice.

Of course, please read them as if
we weren't talking only to ourselves.

No, it's not...

...sweet, nothing sweet about it, but somehow it wants to stand, have even an entirely idiotic sky, imperceptibly, or in silence.

Who was it who was saying not too long ago they don't hold grudges, though their mother and brother do?

Well, I do, but can count them on the fingers of one hand, or maybe an octopus's eight. Some, if not most, are trifles. It would take a magician, or a cloud of psychoanalysts to make sense of the particular pain. Or, the collection might explain, add rhyme if not reason, actually paint a portrait of the wounded, having nothing to do with the wound.

Some psychoanalytic minefields are not even recognized until they explode decades later, or discerned only as a constellation of tender goats. *You can do this to me, but not that.* Let's clear the air for all time.

The best revenge is memory.

YOU KNOW…

…who you are
if you're still alive.
If you recognize yourself
I'll never admit it.

Just a little (harmless)
exorcism. If you're dead
it can't hurt you.

If you're certain
I'll deny it.
If, if, if.

Not finding yourself?
Don't worry
I haven't forgotten you
or maybe I have.

TIME

It's time to make up our minds –
what and whom we like and don't
(with room for revision and generosity, of course).

Not decorous, *sauvage*.
Speak your mind!

What a time, We've stopped believing
in classical anything. That's good, perhaps
and a salvé for bats, except for belief

in bat-shit crazy!

Revenge is simply...

...that I withdraw my misplaced affection
and see you as you are. It hurts to do so.
It hurts me more than it does you.
That's the problem, nothing hurts you.
You say there's nothing wrong with me.
That is wrong. You are wrong with me.
(Is there an echo in here?) And it matters
not at all. Revenge is nothing more
than a silent, invisible scowl.

Where Have All the Idols Gone?

Keep your friends close. Keep your enemies closer.
Keep your idols far, far away.

I do better staying away
(as does everyone).

"If you didn't built them so high
they wouldn't fall so low."

someone said, years ago.
Oh, it was my wise social worker.

What did she know!
I want my idols whole, savory

as all things *entières*. I want to be soothed
by belief, companioned, shy as a meerkat.

Don't come near me, don't shatter.
We live our fantasies, and love them.

Fantasy is life-sustaining.
Don't out-grow!

The problem is, the analysts are human.
They're as human as the analysands.
(And, when you realize that, you're cured.)

The poets are human. Even the critics are
some, many if not most, indistinguishable
from the poets.

It's a big problem. There are no heroes.
There really aren't any. There is not one.
None. (An idol of mine was a stickler...)

I refuse to think about politicians. Are they
even the same species? Celebrities? Please don't
annoy me with weird degradation products.

I'd imagined there were real, living parents
even if I had none. Not one. I imagined
there was such a thing as grown-ups who *knew*.

How painful and poignant the longing.
How godless we are. Not disillusion, but truly
the dissolution of illusion.

DUE COURSE

OK, so you don't like them.
No problem, just wait for them to die.

May not have to be a long time
or for some other disaster to befall.

Off the table, out of the chair
expunged from the guest list for sure.

Forgive and forget.
Forgive but never forget.

I'm not sure there's such a thing
as forgiveness anyway, just changes of weather

new volcanos elsewhere, fanciful
triumphant escape, artistry of survival.

Or, rave indifference as nature
takes its recourse.

Do not...

...mistake this palsied hand
for one that cannot strangle you

this palsied brain
for one that cannot think

lucid thoughts about your contempt
subtle and otherwise.

Revenge will be you too
will forget your name, your keys

your palsied thoughts and memories.
You too will, if you're lucky.

SURELY

You will not be spared
if I'm in a bad mood.

No one will, especially not
those I love the most.

They're never spared
day in and day out.

Those loved the most
are spared the least.

Not All...

...injury requires revenge.
Some is just sorrow, blameless
someone who *did the best they could*
without malice, or merely call it
'innocent, ignorant fool revenge'.
The pain needs to be particular
not mere disappointment.
It needs to be analyzed, which is
not always an easy task
finding the locus of the insult
the tiny spine. Some monsters
are not really monsters.
They're more just inadequate
and that's really worse.

I

There has to be, let's say
a grievance.

GRRRRRR

I've tried to think long and hard
why we didn't like him, but
we didn't, and weren't very nice about it.

We passed notes whenever he spoke
that read, "Grrrrrr", rolled our eyes, subtly
of course, even giggled a little.

It was fun, and he never knew
armored by (or enamored with)
conceit.

Was it the breathless false modesty?
Self-satisfied sincerity?
What *was* so dislikable?

Sycophantic ingratiating oration?
Faux faux faux!
At least, do it well.

WHEN THINGS BECAME CLEAR

The antique dealer in the Ivy League town
was mustached, elegant enough to inspire.

But one day I knew, I just knew.
The style was wrong – a late revision

curious in itself, the handle replaced
as can happen, the spout, well

clearly I hadn't known how to see.
That bastard, he swindled me!

And, for no reason – I liked it
and would have bought it anyway.

He might have tried to educate
spread knowledge like wildfire.

Instead he deceived with his long
lovely, sublime authority.

I remember so clearly, the way he
constructed the lie, almost a hedge:

"Do you think it's original?"
"I have no reason to think otherwise."

You had a thousand reasons, or only one.
Was it followed by remorse or glee?

Did you need the money old man?
Of course you did. Who buys

that ridiculous old stuff anymore anyway?
It's a simple story, as most are not.

The dealer is undoubtedly long dead.
(Did you take your profit to the grave?)

There's no revenge in saying
Keep the change to a poor thief

and many I'd give my whole heart to.
I suppose I should be glad, after decades

out of nowhere, developing an eye
blinking now with silly rage.

*

A companion story, a curiosity
a rare museum day
when I was to wrap artifacts.

The curator asked, "Early 18th century?"
"Oh no" I replied, casually, not to offend
"At least a hundred years later".

How, I wondered. Blithe, but how it settled.
Expertise clear and spare, no way
they couldn't have known.

I've always wanted to ask
"Were you testing me
to see if I was a thief?"

Uninvited

Was it sadism disguised as wit
or pathos disguised as sadism?

Unbearable disguised as merely
unpleasant? Sour or bitter?

You don't hold a grudge
you are a grudge.

Be a grudge, begrudge.
Was it narcissism, or anxiety?

Envy disguised as superiority?
Loveable grouch, minus the loveable.

Is it just me, or are you
as odious with everyone?

Bitter provocateur, are you
asking someone to finally care?

Don't poke, troll, bait or taunt me
or let me become you.

No, the cat doesn't have fleas.
Something else gnawed your ankles.

You're in the countryside now
with bugs, or maybe a devil collecting dues.

Sorry you almost blew up the house
and broke my favorite knife

danced at midnight like a dervish
appalled the friendly neighbors

talked about sex and exes.
Complained, complained, complained

and accused me of locking my husband
in the basement. Truth is, he fled.

A Faint Smile (!)...

...from the rather severe-looking
woman at the pharmacy
française, naturellement.

White hair but a stylish flair.
Moulin Rouge intellectual.

I'm afraid of them
but know and understand.
Contain the fear, no *klaxonne!*

To be so elegant, so *French.*
So cool or cold, class in a glance.

One cannot help but respond
in kind, like a mirroring mime.
How it confers dignity

for a long moment.
Rester sur son quant à soi.

How to freeze one's head
though I'd rather be disarmingly
friendly.

I ignored her, I imitated her
studied, serious way

chatted up the young clerk
with apologies and gratitude.
I am a stranger.

She'd broken my heart
and now it's fixed.

Holding my Tongue

One for a professional having a hissy fit
whose mercy I'm pathetically at
demanding a movie star's ransom
for not my bad. Be sure, I'll be the one

to let you know if I've misbehaved
when I should hold my breath in shame.
Dear over-priced self-appointed scold
how about a bit of hand-holding in the morass?

Hold, not bite, slap or wring.
Just finish your job, dear high and mighty
ticket taker, bean counter, pettiest of petty
bureaucrats before I fire your ass.

Did I? No, I practically kissed it
and explained, sent more info than Britannica
apologized as if I'd run over a cherished cat.
All was repaired without exorbitance.

PARKED

Parked badly (who has *that* skill?)
and a bus came.

"Are you sure you want
to park like that?" the driver asked
quite politely through the open door.

I looked. "Well no..."

But why are you screaming at me?
Can't you see I can't do any better?
Why are you doing this to me?
I hate you. I'm going to kill you.
Go to Hell you evil bastard.
How dare you scream at me?

The passengers looked on, surprised
at least, enjoying the meltdown
envying the freedom, pitying
the rage.

Dear X,

I must confess we remain traumatized by Y's rudeness during our last visit, especially to me. ...still ruminating as to how character could have been so poorly judged.

And, how are you treated, sweet jewel? Complicit, or a victim? A complicit victim? Someone too cheerful to notice?

Then again, the sad life story, which I'm generally sympathetic to... But, how much was true, or profoundly true, vs. angled creation? We all live our own spins, no? Constitutionally hapless or not, don't we ration our own light and darkness?

Analyzing the complaints, it seems *a woe-is-me, but I don't give a shit* interpretation is the only interface with the universe. If lucky, one has many years to recover from the bruises of the past, albeit with scars.

I was, frankly, so stunned by the behavior that, fortunately, there was no way to respond. Good manners, which are their own form of contempt, were my only defense. Even now, I can extend my sympathies to the full of what pathos is.

The Card

"The card's no good!"

Calm down before you shriek.
It was an expensive purchase
perhaps once in a lifetime
taken 'on approval' before deciding.

"The card's no good!"

I might have been kinder for her worry
but the card was perfectly good.
Just had to get the limit raised
I didn't say, but upped it, lickety-split.

My husband brought them
mountains of business over the years.
They knew him well.

You might want to consider
calming down before you shriek
especially when the patron
feathers your nest with fancy-asses.

I might have practiced
my own aristocratic bearing
that particularly icy, overly enunciated
reprobation with a millisecond of glower.

Calm down before you shriek
and do not try to shame me
that particularly unbearable jab
I am unworthy and should not breathe.

Dismissed or demonized
rendered, as are so many
other.

CHARM

Someone bought 'meritorious' admission:
"You're very naïve."

Photographing a grand banquet:
"You were annoying everyone."

Lunch for three:
"I wasn't talking to you."

The 3rd time *is* a charm!
I'm sorry your nice (nicer than you)

husband died. I'm sorry you
died, too. But, let me say

I've had enough reprimand
by an imperious goddess.

Glad I don't live in your (fancy) world.
collecting admirers like seashells.

Cherish naiveté. It may keep one
honest and kind, if not alive.

Daffy – Dachshi

The Daffodil Festival is a dazzling maze of blooms and unheard-of expertise. Who knew this sublime universe existed? Well, I'd won the photography prize the year before, for an image of, yes, a daffodil.

Kindly, a younger associate of the Garden Club asked if I might like to be a judge this year, and took me to meet a venerable senior member. Not a judge of the daffodils, of course, as if Wordsworthian perfection could be conferred, but of photographs of daffodils: the ephemeral metamorphosed to nearly eternal.

She was an older woman, unadorned but handsome, perhaps a bit severe, sitting in a comfortable chair. Hearing her apprentice's concise appeal, she lowered her head and looked away. There she froze. There was nothing less to say.

Is dismissal worse than contempt? Had I ever encountered this particular variety? We'd been too surprised, or polite, to laugh. I might have said, "Who raised you?" but already knew. And knew other members of her illustrious family, including some of their impossible-to-avoid-not-so-secrets. But, it was hard to take true offense. I'd been standing beside her, anonymous as a dandelion, and she never looked up.

*

Preferring the 'hybrid vigor' of strays to purebreds, I had to admit our downstairs neighbor was adorable: a longhaired dachshund puppy duly named Dachshi.

Once, when his dog walker was indisposed, he became mine for an afternoon. We took a little walk around the neighborhood, happily prancing in the grass, then came home and played. After a while, I returned him to his crate. (Why it's not called a 'cage' is beyond me.)

And there he sat. "Dachshi?" In a single, fluid movement he looked down his long puppy muzzle and turned his head away. There was no mistake. I took him out again and we romped a bit before a treat and re-confinement. He repeated the performance.

Is there special laughter for astonishment? How did a seemingly sophisticated gesture belong to a cute little pup? Hardwired? Instinct never so subtle. Rather than merely being rude, had the old woman inhaled her own sneer scoff mock loft haught, and relapsed to a canine brain?

BASQUIAT

No reason to dislike her, her particularly
though not uniquely frozen face.
Nor the husband on his last legs, or appearing to be.
He, no doubt, was the *macher,* or was he?

Neither a hair out of place, nor a word.
Never a failure to appear
in the paper, seen about, as if accidental.

A Basquiat in the dining room of a vacation house.
Maybe she's nice, her causes are.

Maybe it's envy, not for the things – they're silly
and if only Basquiat hadn't been discovered
maybe he'd still be alive – but her carriage
that conveys absolute certainty.

Hold your head high is good advice for the anxious
down-trodden, angry, defamed and modest.

Maybe it's unfair. Frozen in her own pale gray shadow
maybe she bleeds like everyone else
in spite of her wealth, or all the more because of it.

Not one's fault for having been born rich.
Perhaps it's even harder to be the artist
of your own fortune, worthy, worth
anything.

SMART ENOUGH

Being smart is not enough
especially prefacing smart things
with lilting things. Nothing
like being a genuinely smart
lilting know-it-all. Oh, *coo.*
Go ahead and *coo.*

You were nice enough until
you weren't, until the project failed
or so you thought, nonsensically
officious beyond reason
then shattered like a precious vase
a vagrant wind blew off the RSVP.

You had to be smart enough
to know how to stab my ancestors.
Who gave you inside information?
Lilting unkind witch, tell me how
I failed, my burnt soul failed.
And tell me the cure hadn't worked.

The Contractor

He wiped his feet x2. A tidy prophecy.
Little did I know it was like a tic
a dog sitting for a treat.

Rhapsodized about learning
to read old houses from his father
falling in love with 'patina'.

Local, old world, old school
he had me hammer and nail.
But, every time I look I see

the positively shitty job he did.
Only a picture tells, or a hundred, literally.
This was the beauty of a lost century

in his pudgy hands. At least fill the holes
my restoration heart, with something other
than bullshit. It was the fabric of home

I wanted. To sit and sway and watch
treetops twinkle behind old glass.
$65 to drive to Home Depot

for a screw? Screw you!
I could have taken a limo.
None of them match anyway.

As sorry as I feel for myself
I feel sorrier the little place, never
to return to benign neglect.

"How are you?" a friend asked.
"Fine, except I want to kill
my contractor." "Oh," she said

"Everyone wants to kill their contractor."
But, then her husband died, and I
shriveled in my trivial, lifelong

salvage of ruin, longing for greater
meaning of antiquity, strange solace
of repair, of a world in so much pain

a brass hinge to restore a cabinet
no one can reach, a useless metaphor.
(Are they all?)

PARTY

My father thought FDR saved the country.
Take it from there. I'm a cradle-to-graver.
They say it's as intrinsic as eye color.

But, they kept calling, calling and calling
my sick husband. "Please take him off your list."
I said, nicely I'm sure.

"No, we have to talk to him." "No, you can't
talk to him, he's sick." A few rounds later
they were funning me, not at all nicely.

Not nice enough to be a Dem at all. Nor I.
With apologies to gators and crocs
I'll rip the skin off your off your reptilian body.

I'll pour milk and honey, make that buttermilk
all over your headquarters, add olive oil, too.
How's that for terrorism?

I'll get your arrogant little shit volunteer
ass fired as soon as I write a big fat check
in your name to the Repubs or

like a Jewish alcoholic in recovery –
"Send if I relapse" –
to the American Nazi Party.

This Really Happened

It was a fancy, crowded, pretentious art fair. (Is there any other kind?) After struggling through the melee, we made it to the snack bar where my husband went to stand on line, and I managed to find a small, unoccupied table by a far window, with 2 free chairs. There was a view of the courtyard and a famous monument.

A woman with a camera came near, neither young nor old, casual dressed and nondescript. I doubtless looked like I was hovering over the empty chair, or at some point may have indicated, subtly or otherwise, I was actually trying to save it.

She turned and said in an unidentifiable accent, "Don't worry, I don't want to sit down. I'm taking a picture of the monument. You're not attractive enough to sit next to."

My blank or grave astonishment finally broke. "*What* did you say?" She looked distinctly satisfied, and walked away.

PAGE RAGE

@ International #BLM protests following the death of George Floyd:

Lauri Robertson
June 9, 2020 · 👥   ···

I feel like my generation is coming full circle, and handing over the baton. Here's Joan Baez in Newport in 1968. And, here's a wild, dragon orchid from the secret garden:
https://www.youtube.com/watch?v=cgCJ8UU41tw

As a member of the generation being forced to receive yet another baton for races that shouldn't even have to be run because nobody bothered actually running the fucking race and crossing the finish line once the starting shot was fired, keep your Joan Fucking Baez and live up to the fucking promise you made everyone.

3y   Like   Reply

Lauri Robertson
▓▓▓▓▓▓ Please don't be mean... You might want to consider there's a species problem... I am just plain happy to see life coming to life...

3y   Like   Reply   Edited

Dear Page Rage,

"Fucking JB" has done more for social justice everyday of her life than you will do in your whole life.

P.S. I'm not angry, I just like the word *fucking*. My mother was shocked when I used it as teenager, and used it back at me, which was shocking. I use it for emphasis, so no one will think I'm an elite, effete, privileged, fucking white man.

Bites & What I Should Have Said

"Keep a civil tongue in your head."
                                        –Julie Mutti

                    *

Maybe that's why your mother didn't love you!

                    *

You're so bright
it's a shame you never did
anything with your life.

                    *

Did you miss your therapy appointment?
You better call your therapist.
Is your therapist on vacation?
Did your therapist fire you?

                    *

I'm sorry you got fired.
It couldn't have happened
to a nastier guy.

                    *

Human toxic waste dump
with an emphasis on dump.

*

You have to tailor
the answer.

It takes decades of thought
not milliseconds.

And then, and then
one doesn't care.

II

"From childhood's hour..."
  – Edgar Allan Poe, "Alone"

Roxanne

I was visiting Brigitte – *Bree-jhitte* – and her brother, *Patrice,* a name I'd never heard before. They were exotic because they were from Belgium.

The building was not exotic though, a post-war complex, pinkish and unadorned, not even deco like ours, but with a large concrete terrace over the garage that several apartments opened onto. You could ride a bicycle from end to end in seconds. There was an umbrellaed table, chairs, plants etc., and a small rubber pool.

I was friends with Brigitte and Patrice because my bedroom window faced the terrace, and we chatted on and off across the narrow back alley between us for as long as we were allowed to stay up. Perhaps I was 8, Brigitte a year older, and Patrice one younger. He was cherub-faced, and had his own loaf of bread that he was allowed to eat anytime, with jam.

Sometimes I was invited over for tuna fish sandwiches, which were everyone's favorite. The first time, looking back at my window, I was shocked to realize that while I saw them, the terrace, and all that went on in bright light, from their vantage I was no more than a small gray face behind a rectangular screen.

Roxanne's grandmother lived in one of the other terrace units, and sometimes Roxanne visited. She was chubby, about our age, with stringy hair.

That day, she assaulted me.

Of questionable manners and a bit feral in my own way, I understood talking back or sulking, a targeted hissy fit, recalcitrance, or whining "No fair!". But jumping/tackling/physically assaulting someone, anyone, large or small, was completely beyond me. I knew there was such a thing as 'war', in which there were guns, and something called 'boxing' as a kind of vulgar but choreographed entertainment. But didn't otherwise understand this human possibility, certainly not in our world of peaceful, monotonous brick.

I was stunned. I tried to escape but was pinned. My hair was in her fist, and she pulled. How long did it last, this never-before sensation? It couldn't have been very long.

Had I done something to provoke her, which memory now forbids? Was she living with her grandmother? Did I say something? "Where are your parents?" Or was it because I was, yes, an outsider, but the invited guest, the *friend*. What did I know of someone who might not have had friends?

I remember nothing more about that day these sixty-plus years later than utter surprise which, fortunately, has never been repeated. Neither in the street nor a bedroom, on a refugee ship or in a bar.

Of Roxanne, I've always thought of *rocks,* her violence embedded in her name and in my brain. I'm not sure if I ever saw her again, brightly lit on the terrace. Was it just her haggard grandmother, watering a geranium? There is only a lucid, lucent memory of what that moment was, the violation, and is in the world, every day, stabbing, crushing, smothering, emolliating.

There's neither anger nor revenge, now or then. Perhaps only a brief fantasy of where she came from, and what she might have become.

Brigitte and Patrice moved away a couple years later. I visited them once in Maryland. My father put me on the bus with a tasty BLT.

I thank even shards of my own family, small and gray behind our screens, for civility and enduring naiveté.

The Cruelty of Children

We played almost every day.
Her mother didn't want me there
not really, not that often
but there I was.

We played lots of things: jumping
on the bed and practicing fainting.
Sometimes sensuous Brownie camera
photos of each other admiring flowers.

And, dolls. Barbie's body was so weird
with shrunken feet and tortured torso.
We knew no real women looked like that.
But, she was popular, even then.

We'd negotiate through a little pile
of clothes between us, piece by piece.
"Can I have this? You can have that.
Can I have this one and that?"

Enthusiasm, persuasion, persistent
steam-rolling greed, one day I
ended up with most of the goodies.
Then she didn't want to play.

Then I wouldn't let her quit – nudged
cajoled, gloated until she curled.
Triumphant as I was, there was
no triumph in beating beaten spirit.

One day she asked if I loved her
mother. I said I did, and she ran
to tell her mother who replied
"Well she shouldn't."

Bullied

In the playground, they called her
"Sloppy Sox". Yes, they were
all stretched out. And the teacher said
her fingernails were dirty.
She remembers, but doesn't
remember caring.

Years later they asked
"Are you a snob?" Was it when
she paid for lunch with her name
on a piece of paper? That's how
they did it, subtly, not to embarrass
someone getting free lunch.

She didn't mind. She didn't know
what they were talking about.
Was it proud bearing or ignorance
that stood out? Fierce adolescent
arrogance, innocence? "You're not
conceited. You're convinced."

THE GIRL SCOUTS

Not that they recruited me
for sex or anything, as it
later turned out to be for some
tender campers back then.

They simply omitted me
my mother in *that place*
as it was called back then
for a very long time, back then.

The Brownies as they called us
"flew up" as the saying went.
When the day arrived
I was not on the list.

It was the other mothers
who ran those things back then
or didn't. Perhaps malice was
as absent as my absent mother.

But, spurned spurs. For a few days
I wanted to join the Jr. Calvary.
I heard there was such a thing
with horses and everything.

Then I simply stayed home
and did 3 badges on my own:
Sewing, something, and
Languages I think, back then.

I showed up at a meeting
with my wares, a goddess awful
wrap-around red-checked skirt
that looked like a table cloth.

Abbie Esterman's mother
put it on and gave it a twirl
twirled like a 50's girl
and they let me in.

Why do I believe now
I smiled then, so deeply
and secretly. So quietly.
Is triumph revenge?

FORBIDDEN

She forbid her daughter to play with me.
I wasn't allowed in their house.
I knew why. How did I know?
Yes, my mother was in *that place*.

Years later I learned her daughter
who turned out to be a thoroughly decent
soul, had not spoken to her in decades.

Oh, there was another in the neighborhood
who didn't like my manners and said so.

Years later I learned she didn't much like
her own daughter's either, enacting it daily until
still a youngish woman, the cancer ate her
body and soulless.

STUPID UGLY SMITH

I don't know if she was stupid. She wasn't in the smart class
in those days of "homogeneous grouping".
And, she wasn't particularly ugly, whatever that means.
Maybe a little gawky, skinny, and her mouth may have hung open a bit.

I don't remember ever speaking to her, or her to us.
We must have known her name from gym class
with those awful blue pantaloons, skirtlets, and roll call:

"Smith".

When or why we added, "Stupid, Ugly" I don't know either.
But, it stuck. Did we call her that? Was there ever any reason
to speak to or about her to anyone? Or, only among ourselves
for no reason. I don't think she knew.

Let us all be ugly enough to quell the qualms of Aphrodite
hear our names in their rightful versions, elocuted without prejudice
stupid enough to be oblivious to the cruelty of Jr. High School girls.

My Mother's Social Worker

Might you have considered
it was not about forgiveness
that it was the daughter
who needed rescuing
and was the one
worth saving
first?

How Not To Be a Psychiatrist

You change their course by a few degrees,
and they land on a different planet.
                              ~ Ernst Prelinger, PhD

I wouldn't have hated him
so particularly
if he hadn't had power over me
and the privilege of showing it.

Women around a table smiled
at an anxious teenager interviewing
for the halfway house:

social workers, the squirrel-faced director
my saccharine mother
wanting *only the best for [her] daughter.*

And he, the doctor
with a parade of questions
I answered as best I could.

"Yes, I missed a lot of school."
"Yes, my mother was
incompetent, incapable, incomplete
spent the days smoking in bed."

Infantile, incapacitated, inadequate.
At the helm he interrupted to say
"But, I *like* your mother."

Diagnostic provocation
or pure sadism?

The room was dumb
before daggers melted my cheeks.
"Well, you can have her."

I thank him neither
for a lifelong grudge, which is my own
nor the pulse to bend the arc of fate
but the sterling lesson.

And, what was he doing handing out
birth control pills to all the girls?

"No, I want a diaphragm."
To cycle with moods, to have a body
that learns itself, erotic leaps, and moons.

The Neurologist

I came a long way to see him
dressed as the grown-up I'd almost become
to ask what killed my father.

"I was interested in your father's case."

I came to learn, his alphabet of choices:
this one, that one, another. Genetic?
"Yes, or contagious." All of them
I came to learn, years later, wrong.

"Your mother failed to get the *morbid anatomy*."
"Well, of course there was something
wrong with him. He was married to her."

I came from far away to see him.
No longer the 16 year old daughter
of a man who'd taken years to die.

I came to learn
interested in your father's case

more caustic than the old neurologists' joke:
"Where is the lesion, what is the lesion
and what's for lunch?"

"The Transmission of Irrationality"

I watched those famous folks turn to dust.
Whom I didn't idolize, exactly, but shivered near.
It did take years. Now I can't remember a name.
Yes, the moniker simply evaporates.

Regarded so carefully – *the admiration gaze.*
I never should have put them in The Pantheon.
Now I recite the alphabet for a cue.
Yes, a first name, of the wife only.

They wrote a book I thought was my life.
Had I made it to the other side
worthy of a collegial balcony seat?
How far does shame fall? How they fell

appropriating 'primitive' art, and proud of it.
Still, no last name has arrived, and dust
has gathered on the audience alike.
How much damage they did.

He was merely human, and not a very good one:
bombastic, arrogant, wrong for so long.
A finer colleague's nonchalance:
"Oh, he's always been like that."

I had a vision of flying from the balcony.
Do not lend the unworthy your yearning.

Ruffians

"John, 17 months, for 9 days in a residential nursery"
A film, 43 minutes, 1969

The sympathy was supposed to be for John
abandoned, as they did in the day
by mother in her 'confinement'.

Day #1, John eats well. I remember so clearly.
It goes downhill from there – protest, rage, despair.
England, perhaps of course, not exactly Dickensian.

A.k.a. an orphanage, where cups were banged
with raucous spit and snot.
"John was no match for these ruffians."

My sympathy wandered. C'mon John
get fierce, get feral, make friends, join
the ruffians. Just pretend it's a boarding school

in grainy black & white, almost old enough
to be motherless like the upper class.
He was aggrieved and bereaved, pissed

when she returned. Well...
How wrong is classist in the abattoir
of theories we teach for decades?

Oh, and I was a ruffian, I forgot to say.
A gentle, wordy ruffian. Worthy, please.
Some of us are, just a little rough.

Hail to the ruffians!
How about some longitudinal follow-up?
Apparently John did just fine.

Dear friend(s)

from about forever ago
ever since we knew the word
and who, decades later
decided to trounce me
once, or twice.

(I didn't read the 2nd missive.
It's still sitting there).

Well, heartbroken, yes, well
yes, I always knew
you were more than a little wacky.
But no, I ain't goin' there
in rain, sleet or snow.

Life is imperfect
if you haven't figured that out.
We are imperfect and
not every weird or otherwise flaw
can be stitched.

So, years later still, I haven't
forgotten you. No, not that shallow
but make peace with sorrow
failure, rage a given, silence
and the tacitly irreparable.

Did I think there was more
capacity for humor, loyalty, depth?
I did.

MOTHER'S DAY

There was nothing to forgive.
Forgive water for pouring through your fingers?

Nor revenge, except perhaps survival.
Lacuna still lacuna. What life is without?

But gratitude, for lack of convention, infantile
goodwill now transcendent, for the other

somewhat saner half of the gene pool.
Still lacuna, star-crossed, but kindness

surviving deprivation. What is missing remains
unknown. *If I have no heart, it's because you broke it.*

Finding heart, a little imperfect, discursive heart.
Not even hard now, just a sigh.

TRAIN

"How did you get to Vassar?"
"I took the train."

"Uh, I mean, your father was dead
and your mother was... How
did you manage to get to Vassar?"

How did you get to Vassar?
How *did* you get to Vassar?
How did *you* get to Vassar?
How did you *get* to Vassar?
How did you get *to* Vassar?
How did you get to *Vassar?*

"I took the train
like everybody else."

BITES & WHAT...

Is it hard or easy
to write with one's hair
down, hackles up?

*

Niceness and civility
are defenses
thank goodness.

*

At dawn I speak of you
not you, just your heart
or one you broke
for no reason.

*

Surviving one's history is one thing.
Coming to terms with it is another.

*

What I've learned
from writing this book:
You may not know the true
depth of the wound
until your scalpel
explores it.

III

Reminds Me of Uncle Dave...

...not really my uncle, my mother's first cousin
son of a suicide (his father), nephew of a suicide
(his aunt, my mother's mother, my grandmother)

in his later years, after surviving a cardiac arrest
on Martha's Vineyard (MV 911 was proud of that!)
to die at least a decade later of stomach cancer.

Not that you need to know.

He asked me, nearly on his death bed, did I think
it was OK to stop treatment, meaning the nasty kind.
The shark cartilage through his PEG didn't seem to do

much harm
or good.

He told me a story of upset.
Some story of (minor) conflict
with boys in the neighborhood.

It was a story of irrational
burning rage. I'd have found it
a little paranoid, except he did too.

How the brats horsed around
mean to be sure, how they
mocked his crooked eye

from an aneurysm in his youth.
Nothing like baiting
a defenseless old man.

All pretty stupid if not harmless
except it burned in him
like "The Tyger"

bittered his aromatic pipe.
He'd have killed them
if he wasn't law abiding

but couldn't name the monster.
It reminds me my own little stories
are dull pimples.

Why?

Why cheat when you didn't need to?
Or, some unknown need crept
to self-immolate?

Poverty, it couldn't have been.
An aging aunt in the attic
addicted to absinthe?

There's no mistake you did it
falsity forgery fraud
leaving admirers aghast.

Scholar, pioneer, seminal all the more
over time. Accomplished, famous
rhymes with blemish.

Greed, just greed, who knew
it could exist for nothing
but to squander dignity

and disappoint the children.

RERUN

He cheated on his wife. You
cheated on him with someone else.
He cheated on her with the next
then married again. Confused? Yes.
He had a small penis. Had it gotten lost?
Had he forgotten it somewhere?
They all got together and laughed:
"Where's the other half?"

PATIENT RIDDLES

Kindness kills
because you have a gift to give.
Generosity kills. Baffling, isn't it?

Someone, I forget who, or why
said, "Your solicitous kindness."
Solicitous kindness still stings.

Was I trying to butter someone up
because I wanted something?
Don't we all, and call it manners?

Envy kills. I used to envy
those with tragic loss
of what I never had to lose.

The more you give the more
I'm reminded I have nothing to give.
I am nothing.

ORCHIDACEOUS

Well I was just trying to be folksy
telling the fancy florist I saw
"these ones" in the grocery store
because I had, and may have been a little
concerned about delivering bad news.

"These ones" he repeated, with condescension
to blight a hot house. "You didn't see *these ones*."

"Yes," of course I should have said
 "a *dendrobium*". Or was it a newly mass-
marketed *phalaenopsis,* in a little ceramic pot
reusable for an herb or two.

(Or was I just gloating about the price
and deserved a little withering?)

Lunch

Once a week we brought our lunch
to the lunchtime seminar.
At an exact time, told by her watch
she ate. At some point we began
to watch her, and wait. Watch her watch
her watch and wait, week after week.

Watch, then eat. At some point
she began to watch us watching her
her eyes roving then not, fixed
on an invisible apparition
mouth open in hesitation
(or was the time not exactly right?)

Watch watch wait wait eat eat.
Alliteration had nothing to do with it
or everything, repetition, a heartbeat.
Was there reason, or was she just
strange? We thought so, watching
and waiting, alliteration just malevolence.

.

The Commission

He quit, finally, after years
of good intention, trying (and it was trying)
being called naïve. (He was that, too.)

Some tides only go in one direction
and it was going with great contention
greed, ethical squalor, stupidity of course.

He finally said, "I couldn't stand the aggression."
Whose aggression? The shrill woman
omnipresent by extenuating circumstances?

Clients hollering for hides? The rich
who 'glittered when they walked'?
"No," he said, "My own."

HIGHLAND

It was the 60's. Let the 60's come.
They hadn't yet to Highland.
My aunt Ruth needed help.
Hers had found a better job
and refused to return.

The new woman was perfectly
nice, bristling silently.
We talked as she was ironing
doilies, about her anti-war stance
feminism, unspeakable sexuality.

How silly she would have looked
in a uniform; a doily for a hat
a doily for an apron. Bring on
the 60's. Aunt Ruth told me
not to talk to the servants.

"She's not your equal."
"Of course she's my equal."
"That's not what I meant.
She's not your intellectual equal."
"Neither are you."

Before the 60's came and went
Aunt Ruth let me have the can
of tuna, not the salmon. Before
salmon was no longer a rarity.
Clothes, she said, should fit

have neither stains nor holes.
She called an exterminator
because she saw a bee.
Oh the 60's finally came
to the dismay of her friend:

"Who would have thought I'd be
this old and have a half-brained servant?"

Housekeeper

Why should this woman
a woman, of course
week after week clean

a toilet she's never peed in?
And, in good cheer.
For an hourly rate

lower, I assure you
than I've ever worked for
in my entire life

(except as a teenage babysitter
more than half a century ago).
Constitutional good cheer.

I tried to give her a raise
but she refused. Oh, last year
she compromised a little

"à cause de l'inflation".
Oh labor, oh labor!
Honest work is honest work

in my book. Some more
honest than other.
Would that good cheer

came easily, to the whole
planet, really. To the
burden of honesty.

If Necessary

The patient didn't want the black doctor
a dignified woman who'd made her way.

I must have ruffled fiercely, soon
ordered to the director's office.

The patient's mother had called to complain.
Somewhere in there he had his say

"I'm not a racist, I'm just scared of them."
The doctor said it was OK. It was not.

The director asked, "What if a psychotic
Vietnam Vet with PTSD didn't want to see

an Asian doctor?" "The history's rather
different here, wouldn't you say?"

"How far do you want to take it?
"To The Supreme Court, if necessary*."

What I didn't say, "What if he didn't want you
because you're a kike and dyke and a stutterer?"

*That was 32 years ago. Whom do we go to now?

Dirt

He dumped the dirt. He just dumped it, from a dump truck, on the sidewalk. Not in the front yard where it was supposed to go, which was a few feet away. Why, I don't know. I begged and pleaded, shouted. He dumped it anyway, and drove off. Not a small pile of dirt. My husband, who'd been out at the time, called the boss, man to man, as the saying goes. It was a long time ago. Exasperation and bewilderment have ended. What followed has not.

I had the bright idea to walk to the small high school a couple of blocks away. It was a magnet school for students interested in the arts, so they weren't 'gerrymandered'. I went to the principal's office, explained my dirt problem, and asked if any of the kids might want to earn some money. I was soon introduced to 2 boys who, after school, appeared at my door. And they worked, for several hours, with a garden shovel and a snow shovel, shoveling the dirt from the sidewalk into the yard.

I paid them $10/hour each, which was sterling for teenagers a quarter of a century ago. And, drove them home. Up the block, and over the hill. Not far, a mile or two at most. "Turn right." "Turn here." "Left at the light." I'd lived in that small city for nearly 20 years, and had never been down those streets.

Should I have called it "soil"? OK, it was soil, for our very nicely redone yard with granite curbing. Should I have said the kids were black? OK, they were black, in America, our America. I don't remember their names or faces, only that they were earnest and jocular, and lived a million miles away.

NYC Subway

I don't tell too many lies
but did that day.

Fumbling with a new camera
right out of the box

I took her picture.
She demanded I erase it.

I didn't know how, or so I said.
Thinking Evans' stealth

graven images, theft of soul.
She finally huffed away.

So many years I rode
in the roar of those numb

faces with every vein
of humanity exposed.

I still have her likeness
putting on lipstick.

Wouldn't she like
to see herself so young?

Then a man came
up to me and said politely

"People don't like it and
someone will kill you."

BITES &...

Happy New Year.
I just want you to know
I've forgiven you for being
a total asshole.

*

I used to feel annoyed when I told a religious
person that I'm an atheist, and they replied,
"That's OK, God loves you anyway." Now, I'm
glad to know I'm covered.

*

I'm going to church
with our Catholic neighbor
to pray for something not so good.

*

I was so mad I threw
a piece of plastic
into the regular garbage
instead of the recycle.

IV

"What you would rather be
dead than is gonna change."

— Angela Holder

MALADY

"Do I deserve this? I suppose I must.
I wouldn't be here otherwise. Was there
a moment when I actually chose this?
I don't remember, but there could have been."

– Elizabeth Bishop, "Crusoe in England"

As if I'd swallowed a starfish
whirling a bit. No, I'd have
noticed that, even a tiny one.
Too salty, emblematic.

Or, maybe a small hedgehog.
One could have crept down
while I slept, and not woken
even the vigilant cat beside me.

Lovely little creatures
spines softer than a porcupine's
certainly when slicked back
but do they stay that way

or bloom, like every malady?
Now I think I'm dying. Well
of course I'm dying by the day
and night, full of chattering mind

that once seemed so important
like everything else, everyone else.
No one can figure the cause
except that it might have come

from too much doctoring
(the doctor said) some months ago.
Scans and scopes can't discern a furry friend
or sweet or horse chestnut shell down there.

But, there's pain, fire and explosive weight.
There's dull and gnawing, radiating piquant
queasiness just from thinking of the sea.
I cannot run or jump from it

isolate with a sling or splint.
No scalpel dramas or porcelain bowls
annoying descriptions of the particulars.
No salve for what's internal

for what cannot be seen
deeper than ribs or spine
slithering and groaning under each.
Tell me, please, tell me.

In the Doctor's Office

I'd rather be going to the veterinarian
across the street.
Cocker spaniel or cockerel
furry feathery
unable to speak
except with sad or wary eyes.
But, I'm stuck
on the other side
with humans and human doctors
who know too much
and not enough
whose care is doled out
particularly for what can be seen.

THE BODY'S REVENGE

She was a lovely woman
perhaps still is. I just don't know.
I met her in the hospital.

She had a lovely name:
Lucretia, Leticia, Louella, Ludmilla, Lucinda.

She was yellow, and of good cheer.
We shared our thoughts

about the hospital menu, watched
different TV shows, slept
with a thin curtain between us.

Her husband was nice, too.
He came after his shift.

Bright yellow, *Autoimmune,* I heard
through that gauzy, sliding veil.
The body attacking itself.

Autodidact, Autobiography, Autocorrect
Autoerotic, Autopilot, Autograph.

I was allowed to walk around the halls
but forgot to look at our shared door
to see her last name.

Or, was it right not to tender
momentary intimacy in our long lives?

Why am I thinking of her now?
I, witness, my misfortune
relatively minor.

Better to leave that long moment
to haunting anonymity?

Not to cry out, *But she was my sister.*
I have to know.
I think of her every day.

Autoimmune, bright yellow.
The body attacking itself.
When I left they were transferring her.

The body's revenge.
But for what?

Educational Quartet

He told a very lengthy, very sad story.
A dying aunt, cared for down to her
last noodles and toilet paper. Tears.

Then he asked for medication
in the vernacular, *drugs*.
"I'm sorry, we don't prescribe
those here." And that, courtesy
of the rules, was the truth.

"Then what the Hell are we doing here?"
"I don't know, what are we doing here?"

*

"So you went to jail and were clean
for 3 years. Why, after all that time
would you pick up again?"

He looked at me as if I had 3 heads.
Et tu, Cerberus? Hound of Hades.
Who am I to prevent the dead

from flying high, evading the crypt
for molecules of joy I'll never know?
"Because," he said, "I'm an *addict*."

*

There was a boy who fooled me
good, maybe fooled himself, too.
Father was bewildered. Only
the hysterical mother knew.
The pharmacist had to clue me.

*

Wiser with the next, next time
with the next. The story plausible
sympathetic, *sympathique*
then incredible, *incroyable!*

I let her shower me with society
manners, the beach house
a subtly crafted bribe?
Was it a plea or a threat?

A husband's sanguine confusion
or collusion? I felt a cryptic smile
for my stalwart refusal, reprise
shame for sadistic denial.

I heard she died sometime later
and didn't ask of what.

All Men are Cremated Equal

Not revenge, at least not mine
though I didn't enjoy his arrogance
or neglect of those less important
which wasn't as immediately apparent
as his onstage charm.

He was, a fellow student said
"The Professor So and So Show
and one I've seen too many times".

Not known revenge, but he was stricken
and had only a 5% chance.
"Well," he's reported to have said
"I've never been less than top 5% in anything.

He died just the same, right smack average.
Maybe he forgot to consider the standard deviation.
All men are...as the title says.

Who can say what happened then.
His family went on.
Some may even have flourished.
New royalty ascended.

Post-Covid

> "We make our meek adjustments"
> — Hart Crane

Different for us old folks, y'know.
We never really came out of it.
Something paralytic or dangling
like an unreachable cobweb.

There's the luxurious fantasy
that we'll always get back to 'baseline'
as if waiting for a sniffle to go away
or a cleanly broken arm.

What about a terrible accident
where one is never quite the same?
Adapt with wisdom and grace.
Learn a new chapter or self.

We're still shy, and have misplaced
a couple of years. Wanderlust
has become agoraphobia, the grocery store
an adventure, and oddly satisfying.

Invent a new self, with different limbs
as if there is continuity, as if there is time.
I think of our friend Tom saying
not 'remission' but 'intermission'.

MEDICO-LEGAL AFFAIRS

– in memory of Angela Roddey Holder (1938-2009)

No matter what they say
about wanting their deaths
when the time comes
they want to live as they are able.

Stuck in a wheelchair. Stuck
in an iron lung. Purgatory
of a recalcitrant body
So much for 'living wills'.

"If I don't know you
put me down." she said.
"But, what if you still like eating
chocolate and petting the cat?"

"I don't care. Put me down."

The poison may be ready
but you will not be. No more
than the gummed mouse
fleeing the cat.

If you can still sing
(as badly as ever). Even dance.
Hold hands in the dark.
Sensation for sense.

The petite white haired woman
looked out at a hundred fresh-faced
medical students and said, in her
singularly flat Southern accent:

"Right now, you think you'd rather
be dead than lose your right arm.
That is going to change."

"What you would rather be dead than
is gonna change."

If I Lay Dying

Things I won't miss:
Studying for a French driver's license.
Feeling guilty for not studying French.
Worrying about being cared for in old age.
Fearing dementia.
Worrying about getting the cat in for the night.
Worrying about you...you, you, you.
Worrying about you dying 1st.
Worrying about what to do with *stuff*.
Suburbs.
Feeling guilty about privilege.
Chipping paint.
Self-consciousness.
Worrying about getting fuel oil on time & the furnace restarting after.
Worrying about the world...world, world, world.
War, war, war...a world too small for war.
Climate, climate, climate. Seas, plastic seas.
Racism, inequity, cruelty.
Cruelty to animals.
Animals dying.
Feeling guilty for eating meat.
Worry, worry, worry.
Feeling guilty for having a housekeeper.
Feeling naïve.
Exercising.
Bureaucracy.
Competitiveness, pretention.
Sports.
Tax.
LIES.

The Right (who are so wrong).

The ravages of age.

Losing friends to the ravages of age.

Worrying about being able to get up the stairs.

Worrying about illness and death.

Lists

BITES...

If I lay dying, it's done.
Done done be done.
Dun dun dundun dun
dadundadundadun.

*

"I've reached my greed quotient."
— Marty Baron

*

Regret is revenge.

V

The desk survived @ 350 years
before meeting you.
Abuse is not 'patina'.

The Tree

It wasn't the tree's fault.
All it wanted was to grow.
But I wacked it, but good.
Topped, and trimmed the sides
severely. Risking life and hip –
You stay at gutter height.

I imagined I was 'pollarding'
as they do in France, making
a beautiful, sculptural thing
like a giant bonsai, with knobs
and fireworks. Truth is, I had
no idea what I was doing.

It was violent, and became
all the more so. I felt sorry
for the tree, but enjoyed it –
sadism late in the season.
It had grown too much.
I'd warned it. What kind

of tree was it? I don't know.
A regular tree. A tree-tree
with leaves and ambition
roots and shoots. All it wanted
was to be a tree. What was it
doing there anyway, inopportune?

Revenge for being
who you are, doing
what you do.

Rats 1973

Something, or everything
makes me think of the rats
we killed for nothing, prowess
in the name of learning
in "Mammalian Physiology".

This is exactly how the experiment went:
we starved rats, 'euthanized', weighed them
cut out their livers and weighed them, too.
The control group got the same
minus starvation.

We discovered
the starved rats lost proportionally
more weight in their livers.

This course was given year after year.
This was learning. That was what we learned
in one sentence. How did we kill them?
Chloroform, I think. They were white
with pink eyes and noses, lab rats.

Where was the visceral horror
ethical objection, or was it convention –
eat the pig not the horse (unless in France).
Where was *my* visceral horror
abstracted for half a century?

I might have wanted to kill them
for something, a cure for cancer
or bubonic plague, ineluctable warmth.
I eat the pig because spare ribs, yum!
I don't eat the horse, my brethren.

Sometimes, the last revenge is mere sorrow.
Did you know that butterflies drink turtle tears?

The Opossum

The cat had seen it run
into the cabinet under the sink.
I didn't know
it was just playing possum
and put it in the garbage can.

To the Boys Who Ate the Swan

She'll be in you forever
I hope you know.
The soul of a swan is indigestible.
And her mate's, too
gliding through the universe
searching.

They have great fidelity.
I hope you know.
Far greater than ours.

And the cygnets, *oh, oh, oh.*

Was it a prank? A silly boy thing?
Or some perverse vengeance
on visitors to the pond
who loved her glide and fidelity.

Or, were you hungry?
I ask at this moment, perversely
boning a chicken for a lovely soup
for the hungry and ill.
Are you ill?

Three of you, the story said.
Budding psychopaths? What next
the family pet? A sad chicken
wouldn't do? Some are pets, too.
I hope we each know.

I hope you ate the feathers as well
and they ruffle inside you
every day.

Quintessence of swan
will follow your semen into your lovers
and into your children, if you have any.
They'll hate you, you'll certainly know.

It can't be undone. The purposelessness.
The curse. Your dreams forever, intractably
haunted by gliding, gliding, gliding.

Old House

There's no revenge for this particular
greed and destruction, the perpetrators
ignorant and proud.

The last time I peered into that beautiful house
it had been gutted like a fish, front to back
entrails, heart, empty as a stolen music box.

Then made 'modern' for thrice the price.
Some say *good, goodbye*. Who needs
the sorry feng shui of history.

Federal mantle, cylindrical root cellar
horsehair plaster? *Bang, bang, bang*
in the middle of the night.

One then another and another and another:
Main Street, Orange, Fair, Pine x3, Trader's Lane.
Judith Chase broke my heart.

Who needs a house with a broken heart?
Who needs a heart at all?

The Bluff

The ocean came
and they remained.

They were rich so they
bought bags of fluff.

The ocean undercut.
I say, "Save Venice

if there's still a chance."
Amsterdam stays.

But scouring the coast
isn't the way.

Your house will
wash up like a shipwreck

or a pack of toothpicks.
The ocean doesn't bluff.

AFTER FORWARD

Riddle

Collecting along the way
there's need to travel lighter
as the trip gets shorter.

The more you take
the less you can take
with you.

LAURI ROBERTSON has written poetry for many years – Adrienne Rich was her mentor. *Revenge* is her 6th monograph. She's a psychiatrist and psychoanalyst, formerly on the clinical faculty of Yale Medical School, now living in Loire Valley, France. She is also a fine art photographer, represented on Nantucket by The Gallery at Four India. laurirobertson.com

www.ingramcontent.com/pod-product-compliance
Lightning Source LLC
Chambersburg PA
CBHW021650120626
46545CB00002B/798